BACKYARD WILDLIFE

Spiders

By Megan Borgert-Spaniol

BLASTOFF! READERS

BELLWETHER MEDIA • MINNEAPOLIS, MN

Note to Librarians, Teachers, and Parents:

Blastoff! Readers are carefully developed by literacy experts and combine standards-based content with developmentally appropriate text.

Level 1 provides the most support through repetition of high-frequency words, light text, predictable sentence patterns, and strong visual support.

Level 2 offers early readers a bit more challenge through varied simple sentences, increased text load, and less repetition of high-frequency words.

Level 3 advances early-fluent readers toward fluency through increased text and concept load, less reliance on visuals, longer sentences, and more literary language.

Level 4 builds reading stamina by providing more text per page, increased use of punctuation, greater variation in sentence patterns, and increasingly challenging vocabulary.

Level 5 encourages children to move from "learning to read" to "reading to learn" by providing even more text, varied writing styles, and less familiar topics.

Whichever book is right for your reader, Blastoff! Readers are the perfect books to build confidence and encourage a love of reading that will last a lifetime!

This edition first published in 2014 by Bellwether Media, Inc.

No part of this publication may be reproduced in whole or in part without written permission of the publisher. For information regarding permission, write to Bellwether Media, Inc., Attention: Permissions Department, 5357 Penn Avenue South, Minneapolis, MN 55419.

Library of Congress Cataloging-in-Publication Data

Borgert-Spaniol, Megan, 1989-
 Spiders / by Megan Borgert-Spaniol.
  pages cm. – (Blastoff! readers. Backyard wildlife)
 Audience: Grades K to 3.
 Includes bibliographical references and index.
 Summary: "Developed by literacy experts for students in kindergarten through grade three, this book introduces spiders to young readers through leveled text and related photos"– Provided by publisher.
 ISBN 978-1-60014-921-4 (hardcover : alk. paper)
 1. Spiders–Juvenile literature. I. Title.
 QL467.2.B875 2014
 595.4'4-dc23
                                                                    2013000905

Contents

Spiders are **arachnids**. They have eight legs.

Spiders make silk.
The silk is liquid
in their bodies.
It looks like thread
when it comes out.

Other spiders
hide and wait for
prey. Some even
stalk their prey.

Many spiders build webs with their silk. The sticky webs catch **insects** and other **prey**.

A spider bites its prey with **fangs**. **Venom** flows from the fangs.

fangs

The spider wraps
its meal in silk.
Then it sucks up
the prey's insides.

Female spiders lay eggs. They wrap the eggs in silk to keep them safe.

Baby spiders are called spiderlings. They **hatch** from the eggs.

Soon spiderlings climb to a high place. They let out their silk and **balloon** away!

Glossary

arachnids—small animals with eight legs and hard outer bodies; arachnid bodies are divided into two parts.

balloon—to float away in the wind

fangs—long, sharp teeth; venom runs through fangs and into prey.

hatch—to break out of an egg

insects—small animals with six legs and hard outer bodies; insect bodies are divided into three parts.

prey—animals that are hunted by other animals for food

stalk—to secretly follow

venom—liquid that can kill an animal or make it unable to move

To Learn More

AT THE LIBRARY

Allen, Judy. *Are You a Spider?* New York, N.Y.: Kingfisher, 2000.

Cronin, Doreen. *Diary of a Spider*. New York, N.Y.: Joanna Cotler Books, 2005.

Marsh, Laura F. *Spiders*. Washington, D.C.: National Geographic, 2011.

ON THE WEB

Learning more about spiders is as easy as 1, 2, 3.

1. Go to www.factsurfer.com.

2. Enter "spiders" into the search box.

3. Click the "Surf" button and you will see a list of related Web sites.

With factsurfer.com, finding more information is just a click away.

Index

The images in this book are reproduced through the courtesy of: Cathy Keifer, front cover, p. 13; FloridaStock, p. 5; Tetra Images/ Glow Images, p. 7; Subin Pumsom, p. 9; Yongsan, p. 11; Peter Waters, p. 13 (small); IbajaUsap, p. 15; Sunsetman, p. 17; Kletr, p. 19; Juan Martinez, p. 21.

Many spiders build webs with their silk. The sticky webs catch **insects** and other **prey**.

Other spiders
hide and wait for
prey. Some even
stalk their prey.